Spiritual Sails

A souvenir for life

Dr. Manvi Chaudhary

BookLeaf Publishing

India | USA | UK

1. Breaking the Bounds

Far and near when darkness instigates to smear,
With no hope and wailing tears when every precious
asset just starts to tear;
When creation starts giving impression of a ferocious
serpent gaudier,
And mind burgeons to a restless bombardier;
When humanity is not even bothered to hear,
And sparkling hues of happiness seems to have broken
heirs;
Then buoyant words are sometimes what our soul needs
to come out of this jeer,
To kill the clouds of gloom with this sharp spear;
Words of great saints when attack our deep intellectual
sphere,
Bouts of happiness then tend to flow through our veins
which lets all our sorrows to disappear;
Scriptures also play an important part in this cochere,
Knowledge is power becomes very clear after going
through these nuggets of cheer;
Spiritual practices help to command the restless mind's

gear,
With taming this jittery thinker life gets warmth even in
a cryosphere;
Adding a pinch of selfless service fills up the void of our
stubborn heart,
Love then starts to flow in life creating an aesthetic piece
of art;
Diving into spirituality with full faith and repertoire,
Life starts to dance in a beautiful attire;
So let's start a brand new journey of blissful optimism,
To break this gloomy gurney of distressful pessimism.

2. Lending our Ears

Listening is an art and science,
After all, it is the basis of a pure conscience;
Intake of good content, is what lets our personality
define,
We become what we hear is the thing we need here to
underline;
What to glean upon is a question which enters into the
picture,
Discerning what makes sense and what not needs now a
fixture;
Best is to hear the words of great saints,
Learning from their experiences can abolish our each
and every constraint;
Getting connected to divine is never a squander,
As righteous path is always what spirituality makes us
confer;
Hearing to the eminent personalities can also be
endorsed,
Listening to their biographies can also be an
inspirational source;

If reading is a habit, then scriptures can be adopted,
Self improvement books can also be concocted;
Idea is to replace negative intake with positive instructions,
Our mind so that reflects only what is an optimistic construction;
When mind becomes pure and clear of despondency,
It then embellishes a spark and radiance of ardency;
Some things in life are not under our control,
But what can be controlled is totally in our bowl;
So, lets take a pledge to consume a blend of goodness,
To relish the taste of sanguinity and its wholesomeness.

3. Conditioning Minds

Hustle and bustle in every nook and corner,
Spasmodic problem of each and every mourner;
This to start and that to evince,
But the mind is always very hard to convince;
So, what can be the possible problem,
And how can we get over to the solution;
All answers are given by "The Shrimad Bhagwad Geeta",
when Arjuna asked Krishna about the same confusion,
The great warrior when found the wind easier to control
than the mind's perfusion;
Krishna addressed this query in a way very refined,
Living in mode of ignorance is the root of this causation
he defined;
Restlessness, stress and anxiety are all its complications,
Adoption of mode of goodness can help us overcome this
web of hopelessness;
Deliberate efforts are needed to take as a first step,
And rest of the things can be seen steadily moving like a
jet;
Chanting pure names of God can help in the process,

Meditating on his picture can add on to the finesse;
Tranquilizing the mind is what this practice offers,
Settlement of chaos is what it promises to proffer;
Acting as a chain to the overwhelmed ignorant mind,
Mode of goodness pursues with this simple practice divine;
Laziness and procrastination then can be easily made to overcome,
Life becomes easy with all tasks done;
Regularity is the key to success,
Impossible is nothing when practice makes the problem regress;
So, let's adopt any one spiritual practice today,
To break the legs of this mind which always makes us slay.

4. Exploring Happiness

Happiness is a state of mind,
Having nothing to do with material world's shine;
It lies in hoarding luxuries is a wrong conception,
This is the locus at which we need to change our
perception;
Deftly it has been expounded in The Bhagwad Geeta
verse two point sixty six,
Joviality prevails when the mind gets a quick fix;
Contentment streams from a composed mind,
Effectuating which requires a strong connection with
divine;
A serene mind is always blessed and happy,
As decisions it makes are never nasty;
A still mind never bewilders the intellect,
Effortlessly it is able to introspect;
When focus is sharp and life gets a quick restart,
Every charge undertaken then easily hits the dart chart;
This is how tranquility plays its part,
Spirituality is the gesture which moves this adorable
cart;

So, why not adopt a devotional practice of our choice,
Be it with meditation or chanting, surely the life will
start to rejoice;
Let experiment and experience be the next mantra,
Cheers of joy will then flow with interesting devotional
algebra.

5. Harmonizing Hearts

Happiness is a state of mind,
Having nothing to do with material world's shine;
It lies in hoarding luxuries is a wrong conception,
This is the locus at which we need to change our
perception;
Deftly it has been expounded in The Bhagwad Geeta
verse two point sixty six,
Joviality prevails when the mind gets a quick fix;
Contentment streams from a composed mind,
Effectuating which requires a strong connection with
divine;
A serene mind is always blessed and happy,
As decisions it makes are never nasty;
A still mind never bewilders the intellect,
Effortlessly it is able to introspect;
When focus is sharp and life gets a quick restart,
Every charge undertaken then easily hits the dart chart;
This is how tranquility plays its part,
Spirituality is the gesture which moves this adorable
cart;

So, why not adopt a devotional practice of our choice,
Be it with meditation or chanting, surely the life will
start to rejoice;
Let experiment and experience be the next mantra,
Cheers of joy will then flow with interesting devotional
algebra.

6. Transfiguring Self

A broken wing never flies,
A simple fact this line very clearly implies;
So as is the case with a broken heart,
It needs a healing touch before it can just restart;
Compiling fragments can sometimes injure the helping
hand,
Which may be of the victim himself or someone else's
loving strand;
But we can surely devise a technique to bind it with a
magic wand,
Inspiring him to take up any selfless service is what we
need to understand;
Lending a helping hand to the ones in need is what he
can be encouraged to do,
Void inside the heart will be filled in just a simple go;
Realizing the pity scenario of the world in dearth,
Helps to understand the value of his own worth;
Offering a helping hand to someone strange,
Fills the heart with bounties of pleasure and positive
impression is left ingrained;

*Every action has equal and opposite reaction, Newton's
Third Law also says,
So why to wait for the things to get perfect to add value
into the life of someone in dismay;
So, let's take a pledge to do one act of kindness every
day,
Not for taking in pride but to rejoice the satisfaction of
riding on a unique picturesque way.*

7. Guarding the clock

"Charity begins at home" we all can easily comprehend,
But then why do we wait the world to first apprehend;
Transition begins with "me" is the fact,
Then why to wait for transposition of the whole sect;
Deep down we acknowledge this verity,
But executing the knowledge is unparalleled necessity;
Life becomes undemanding when we embark on to the
first step,
The business becomes cushy when we take the
responsibility of cutting this web;
Rightly said by Gandhiji that "be the change you want to
see in the world",
The concept of transformation begins when the focus
shifts to "us";
Little drops emulate to make up the big ocean,
Not getting afraid and adopting a tiny bit of change,
should always be the notion;
Skeptic attitude should be kept aside,
Zeal to add on something novice should be kept beside;
Sharing what we learn should be our prime goal,

Waiting for perfection is just going make us fail as whole;
Aim for self-actualization each day should be observed at top,
Do your best and leave the rest is the truth we must always try to adopt.

8. Eliminating the Failure Factor

Time and again we run out of clock,
But then how can we manage our life's stumbling blocks;
Spirituality for self-improvement demands time,
Or time management is the correct word needed here to
define;
Everyone is equally allotted with 24 hours of slot,
But some design success from the same knot;
What is the mystery that needs then to be solved,
To change our future around which our history revolves;
"Busy" word is firstly a myth we need to recognize,
"Chaotic" is instead a correct vocabulary we need here to
scrutinize;
Introspecting ourself for this age-old state of mind,
What new steps can be taken we need here to underline;
First and foremost, we need to understand time,
It's value is more than money and its equivalent to
divine;
A bald man running forth with his long beard in front,
Can be caught only when we are leading in advance to

confront;
Realizing the worth of time comes with sorting of this
twine,
Easily we come out of disrespecting the worth of this
precious Klein;
Destructive to constructive is the way to the sunshine,
Chunks of time wasted adding up to a mountainous
scrap is what we need to recognize;
Working it out for happiness of God can be taken as a
support to condition the mind,
As God is time himself cannot be forgone in good times;
Righteousness in every task if we identify to undermine,
Surely, we can then manage the history, Physics and
Geography of this undefined thine.

9. Age is just a Number

Failure seems to be a very heart throbbing word,
Hostility it creates in our mind now needs to get absurd;
Commonly people are afraid of its arrival,
Sudden influx of whom, is the beginning of a horrible
carnival;
A domino circle is what it is believed to create,
Coming out of that spiral is impossible again and again it
reinstates;
But what if we realize that this word is not a negative
character,
And correction of its image requires a powerful legal
barrister;
Let's take a deep look into our life's biggest failure,
Learning which it gave us should be written today on a
piece of paper;
Now its time to ask one question to ourselves,
The same learning could have been possible with reading
any treatise placed on our book shelves;
If the answer is no, then its time to change the
vocabulary of the word "failure",

*Replacing it with the word "tutor" is needed now as a
positive gesture;
Teachers are not blamed but respected in the society,
Same regard is now needed by this new mentor without
any anxiety;
Learning from him should be now our aim,
Blaming him is not a question that now exists in the
frame;
A man learns for Life should be now our new
philosophy,
Word failure should be completely deleted from our
brand-new dictionary;
Considering failures to be just our teachers,
Will help us come out of the web of this so-called
predator;
As overwhelming comes from a negative attitude
regarding failures,
The vicious circle is only created when the meaning of
the word seems very very horrible;
Moving on is the strength what this conditioning brings
to us,
Failure is just our new mentor, now with everyone we
can easily discuss.*

10. Practicality of Spirituality

Spirituality is meant for old age,
A common myth that has been clarified by every sage;
Spirituality is the journey of soul and not of body,
The Bhagwad Geeta makes this fact clearly imply to
everybody;
"The younger the better" is the phrase we need to always
remind,
Even learning new skills come easily to a person
juvenile;
Spirituality is an art of living and making life divine,
Then why to dive in it at an age when we are frightened
of dying;
With Sanguinity we meet our true identity,
The knowledge which is craved by both old and young
propriety;
Stories of Shrimad Bhagwatam and The Holy Ramayan,
Give beautiful examples of success when righteous path
is followed with enthusiasm;
Many young devotees have set high standards in

devotion,
Prahlad Maharaj and Dhruv Maharaj are some special
mentions;
Dhruv Maharaj was when neglected by his father to
reach his lap,
And his step mother scolded the little one to do first
something great;
Then instead of forcefully insisting his father,
His biological mother guided him to go for devotion
rather;
Within 6 months he was able to attain God,
Spiritual and material riches, with both he was honored
by lord;
For Prahlad Maharaj God appeared breaking the pillars
of the castle,
Protecting him every time whenever he was threatened
by any demoniac killer's hassle;
Children need nurturing from very early age,
Then why to wait to be spiritual on some specific date;
Divine protection is bestowed by God to his devotees
every time,
Child, adult or aged everyone requires it to just simply
outshine.

11. Our Bhagwad Geeta

Very often we have encountered a common perspective
about spirituality,
It has nothing to do with practical life and thus is of no
functionality;
People consider it as a hindrance in performing duties
without knowing its specialty,
Abruptly they jump into the conclusion and just shun its
rationality;
Figuring out that it builds the foundation of our life will
help us to remove this hostility,
Understanding the significance of the same will help us
to break the triviality;
Spirituality is multidimensional which is the only reality,
Spiritual practices, service and good behavior encompass
its overall modality;
Service when done for happiness of God levels up the
work to a very good quality,
And it includes our self, family, friends and the whole
society;
Spiritual practices when increase somebody's mode of

goodness and vitality,

It is then deemed to bring love and affection in the entire humanity;

Building strong relations also require certain level of morality,

Virtues strengthened by following spiritual practices provide us with this beautiful serenity;

Prescribed duties are when performed leaving the fruits of actions in totality,

Then only we experience the complete eradication of stress and anxiety;

It is known to increase focus which is the foundation of high productivity,

Be it personal or professional life it is known to escalate anybody's magnanimity;

So why not give a try to embark on this path of generosity,

To make our life a beautiful garden ornated with jewels of geniality.

12. Spiritual Journey with a Bosom Buddy

In the midst of darkness when we seem to become completely blind,
Remembrance of Krishna then gives a radiance of sparkling light saying, My child! Why do you whine;
He is there for his devotees every time,
Whenever they are struggling and are not fit and fine;
The medium which paves way to his lotus feet divine,
Is The Bhagwad Geeta whose divinity shine in darkness equivalent to bright sunshine;
This knowledge vividly speaks how to restart,
Its learnings guide us to the path on which we need to embark;
An instructional manual on art of living as well as dying,
It's a perfect amalgamation of questions and answers and is always worth buying;
Imparting the pearls of right cognition,
Completely practical and it depicts easy steps to follow in progression;
Arjuna portrays examples of extremes of situations we

face in our lives,
And Krishna plays the role of a rescuer who can take
him out of the web of these twines;
With 18 chapters and 700 Shlokas it's not a mere book
but a precious guide to reach God's abode,
Of which our scriptures mention some of the beautiful
anecdotes;
Here everyone is in bliss serving lotus feet of God,
Super safe and comfortable they are in complete care of
Lord;
It teaches the concept of surrender unto God's divine
feet,
And depicts the science of soul which gives us an
astonishing self-meet;
Joys and sorrows are the sides of the same coin it
teaches,
Leaving the fruits of actions is the beautiful message it
preaches;
Sins are the cause of our sorrows it underlines,
Devoting unto the divine is the solution it always
reminds;
So why not sail through this scripture once in our
lifetime,
Who knows, maybe one day it adds on to the most
valuable asset of our life's timeline.

13. Making a wiser Move

Once upon a time there were two innocent souls,
Knew nothing about the world but were ready to get into
that bowl;
With zero knowledge of right and wrong,
They started their journey which was very long;
One was introvert and the other was extrovert,
With different choices they started to chase the mirage
of a desert;
Chasing the unreal led them nowhere,
And they started to roam just here and there;
Bewildered and confused when the path was not visible,
Reality and truth became simply invisible;
When darkness was at its peak, a ray of hope arrived at
the doorstep of one of the geeks,
Luminosity came in his life in the form of divine words
from their mentor's seat;
How lost he was the realization came up with that divine
knowledge,
Service accompanied by spiritual practices liberated him
from all the bondage;

He was now fine but the other one was still in a charcoal mine,
So, he helped the same with words of wisdom and the same process divine;
Spiritual journey of their mentor became their inspiration,
They can also be like him became a source of positive vibration;
They prayed to Krishna to help them deal with their problems,
Which Krishna answered magically guiding them by a meaningful memorandum;
Divine experiences remained now not so rare,
Fully loaded with God's blessing they both started to glare;
Presence of God was felt by both of them,
With grace of God in the life of those little breadcrumbs;
Turning to God was actually their turning point in life,
Grabbing the opportunity was indeed the key to cutting their complete disguise.

14. Tuning the Temper

Inside the dead of night when dawn seems to have no start,
The colors of happiness when appear to be a portion of just our past;
When motive of living juggle in a mystic jar,
And mind tends to play a set of dissonant guitars;
Wake up to reality then depicts the true purpose of our life waiting to get restart,
And one solution to countless problems "The Spirituality" then answers each and every query of ours;
A close preview of scriptures at that time need to have an immediate attention,
Surrender to divine is required to cut the cycle of this devilish pageant;
Good deeds done to collect some choicest blessings,
Bring Glories of Happiness garnishing our life with a blissful dressing;
Wrong actions taken to accomplish some wildest dreams,
Bring a gloomy scream of sorrows for our future streams;

But when little efforts are made to please God,
Then these tiny devotional packets save us miraculously
from the hit of Karmic Rod;
Mindset to stop the creation of new Karmic cyclic
rounds,
Clear gigantic chunks of dirt of our Karmic sounds;
Better is to leave the expectations of our fruits of actions,
To stop inviting anxieties and frustrations as a sorrowful
reaction;
But sometimes leaving the fruits of action becomes
difficult, as they provide no source of motivation,
So best is to add God in every task that is undertaken;
Working for his happiness will not only make our Karma
Divine,
But slowly and gradually it will take away the wit of
accomplishing material world's false shine;
God is never responsible for any action we perform
whether good or bad,
As he has given us a free will to do what we want,
enshrining his true love for rehab;
Every action has an equal and opposite reaction
scientific principle also says,
Then no point is left to blame the divine for our life
cradle to sway;
When Karma is done for happiness of God with
complete vigor and astound,
Then the supreme promised to cancel the bad Karmic

account of crores of lives in just a click of sound;
Remembering God every time is the key to prevent
getting into upcoming circle of Karmic Whine,
Wavering life will then find a balance and every moment
whether Good or Bad will feel like a gift of Divine;
Happiness in true sense will then be realized,
And flickering pleasure will no longer be able to make us
hypnotize;
Darkness will be replaced not only by bright colors of
hope,
Confidence to become somebody's sunshine will also be
bestowed;
Divinity will then play a melody of harmonious flute,
And heart will rejoice a plethora of blissful pursuit.

15. Panoramic Pedagogy

Appears to be a novice concept,
And places in our minds a newbie percept;
Without even realizing its backswept,
We come to a conclusion to just accept;
But this notion of panoramic pedagogy,
Dates back to times of our Vedic history;
When children were not only made literate,
But overall development was their education's unique
trait;
Soul, mind, body, family and finances were all its arenas,
Just getting a handsome salary alone was not its
complete panorama;
But now-a-days the theory has changed,
Scorching stress and depression, the contemporary
education system has blazed;
Peers just guide their wards to adopt a profession,
Where a huge money flows into their life as an
obsession;
Not realizing the area where the talent lies,
They are forced into the loop of some very complicated

Service should be done in accordance to our nature,
Bhagwad Geeta also hitches the same concept for
everybody's future;
When one works according to their interest to earn
money,
Nothing comes out to be a source of burden for even a
single penny;
Health and relations are automatically then taken care
of,
When happiness starts in a series to flow thereof;
So, let's analyze the holism of education we have
received,
And try to bind up the missing links and get the things
sealed;
For everybody it may not be possible to change their
work,
But interests can be adopted as a side hobby to progress
further;
So, what if we can't completely change our present
situation,
At least we can save the knowledge for the upcoming
generations;
We have to adopt the changes which are in our control,
Something is better than nothing is the quote we need
here to recall;
So, lets don't wait for a specific timing to change,

"Well begun is half done" and the things are now, to us,
not very strange.

32

16. Joviality vs Melancholy

Two words with different meanings in entirety,
One brings happiness and other one sadness in complete polarity;
Chasing the first one and running away from other is a common process we follow,
One is friend and the other is foe is a belief which we again and again swallow;
So, Let's try to dive into "The Bhagwad Geeta" Chapter two for some deep concepts,
And try to find answers in verse fourteen for this age-old percept;
Happiness and sorrows are the part of life it explains,
Expecting either of them not to arrive is inescapable it ingrains;
Just like summers follow winters is a rule of nature,
In the same way joys and sorrows are destined to come is the truth we need here to cater;
Either of them is not designed to get entangled into,
Balance is required to prevent getting into an inauspicious breakthrough;

Wedging into joys makes us careless and insane,
Bogging down to sorrows brings an invitation card to
depression and pain;
Realizing that they are not permanent and are destined
to move on,
Preparation to face both is needed always for life to
carry on;
Being grateful for both will bring the required tranquil,
As even sorrows make us humble is a hidden backfill;
So lets stop escaping either of them to join,
And try to consider them to be the sides of the same
coin;
The day we will learn to stay same in both negatives and
positives,
Life will then rejoice with happiness in each and every
narrative.

17. Contemplating the Nature of Mind

A continuous machine generating thousands of thoughts,
Harbors feelings and emotions with some complicated knots;
Its nature is to always cling towards negativity,
Most of the time it enjoys long sessions of inactivity;
Unstable, restless and flickering are its important traits,
Detrimental information and nasty associations are some its required baits;
Being judgmental it passes on some rapid absurd conclusions,
Always intended to make comparisons and put us in fearful illusions;
It believes in making some extreme levels of attachments,
Complaining every time and is never ready to make even little bit of adjustments;
Like a pendulum it swings into the past and future,
Ruining the gift of present is the phenomenon it always

nurtures;
Obsessed of something new and easily gets bored of old,
Never takes the work to its completion and is very very
bold;
More difficult than wind to control,
Comfort is the mat on which it always wants to roll;
But as nothing in this world is impossible,
As the word itself depicts it as I M Possible;
In the same way mind requires Practice to control its
reins,
As it can be the best friend or best foe "The Bhagwad
Geeta" also untangles this complicated chain;
If trained for redemption it will guide us to the same,
But if taken in a wrong direction its destined to bring us
a bad name;
So why not take advantage of the friendship of this
companion,
To condition our lives into a picturesque canyon;
Small steps taken to do the same today,
Who knows, can bring some delightful results for the
changes we always used to pray.

18. The Giving Guide

With open hands and wide heart,
Joy of giving is a magnanimous piece of art;
Embraces kindness and bestows grace,
Blessings received from sharing are visible on
benefactor's face;
Sharing builds a bond of love,
Brings peace that even outshines the character of a
harmonious dove;
With sharing and caring the hearts intertwine,
A simple act, but yet so divine,
If we care for someone we must share;
But with love and not attachment is the fact we must be
ready to dare,
Now, let's explore this mystery of attachment and love;
The difference between the two now needs to get a
shove,
Attachment is bondage but love is freedom,
The fact to be understood in each and every collegium;
Attachment means to care for some selected individuals,
But love encompasses the whole world to be our own

compendium;
Diffusing love brings jubilation in hearts,
Both giver and the garner rejoice in a protective grill
guard;
Allocating with attachments brings disguise in turn,
As a bag full of expectations, it always asks for in return;
Joy of giving should be a selfless act of service,
Only then it blossoms to a gracious auspice;
It is never associated with loss or stasis,
Rather is known to help cross the bridge of crisis,
Spiritually whatever is shared is known to grow;
So why not use this tool to abolish our age-old sorrows,
Fragrance remains in the hands of those who distribute
roses;
A warm set of memories in hearts it always imposes.

19. The Spiritual Algebra

We must have studied Mathematics in School and
College,
But what it has to do here with respect to the Spiritual
knowledge;
Wait! Wait! We have tried to devise a positive correlation
down the scroll,
So that the probability of understanding the concept
increases up to manifolds;
In math we learn some specific formulas to solve certain
problems,
And only particular theorem is known to fix a distinct
set of questions;
Wrong formula applied will lead to inaccurate results,
And will waste time in going through the complete
process;
Decision making is thus important here at every step,
Analyzing the query beforehand is required as an initial
prep;
In the same way Spirituality works in our lives,
Right attribute has to be applied in some specific

situations which arise;
Let's understand this with the help of a simple example
from "The Bhagwad Geeta",
When Arjuna got confused in the midst of Battlefield at
Kurukshetra;
There he had to fight with his own relatives,
Who were known for doing injustice and always
presenting negative narratives;
But considering compassion to be a divine quality,
He applied the same virtue wrongly without analyzing
that the opposite side was completely guilty;
The reign of Kingdom could not be given to such people
at any cost,
The same hassles are bound to be faced by the populace
in megawatts;
He left his bow and arrow on the ground,
Decided not to fight against his own relatives and felt
drowned;
But then Krishna guided him to fight the war,
In order to place righteousness on the top;
If he won, he was destined to get the kingdom,
But if he lost, then also, he was known to reach heaven
after the martyrdom;
Thus, a beautiful learning can be taken from this topic,
Compassion has to be restricted when it is not needed;
In the same way Anger is also not a form of a good
virtue,

But if it saves someone from danger then it is worth to
apply to prevent a miscue;
So, we always need to choose wisely in our practical
lives,
As the best decisions are made only when spirituality
thrives;
Thorough understanding of scriptures helps in attaining
some positive results,
Spiritual Practices are needed to get a clear picture of
such complicated percepts;
So, this was an overview of the algebra of spirituality,
I hope it will help in breaking the boredom associated
with the worth of this serene path of sanguinity.

20. Count the Blessings

Life is a mixed bag of chocolates and stones,
With sweet moments and trials that test our bones;
But choosing wisely lies in our own zone,
Which can only prevent us from landing in a devilish
throne;
Count the blessings and be happy or count the problems
and be frustrated,
Is the only mantra which we need to harbor to stay
always jovial and gaited;
When we learn to look at our blessings,
Then heart rejoices in bliss of gratitude's dressing;
It will prepare a list of our own benedictions,
And no time will be left to chase for miracles to happen;
The morning sun, the sky so wide,
The soft winds and the whispering smiles;
All will prepare a positivity catalogue,
Wealth and blessings will be comparable to a magnetic
prologue;
So, let us count each of these gems,
The gift of life and good health as a complete blend;

As mind will always cling towards our lack,
A pessimistic blaze it will start to stack;
But the idea is to bring it back to the treasures of life,
And save ourselves from getting into the bondage of a
never-ending strife;
As mind is a seat of only emotions,
Whatever it depicts is only sense perception;
Truth is what scriptures navigate us through,
To stay happy and use human life to create a unique
breakthrough.

21. The Infinite Love

God loves everyone equally up to infinity,
Bounties he shares with us define his pious divinity;
Still he is always left with warmth and affection that
equals infinity,
As infinity minus infinity is always equal to infinity.

God cares for everyone equally up to infinity,
Hiding us from fearful dangers defines his deep
protectivity;
To care is to love is his cordiality,
As infinity minus infinity is always equal to infinity.

God caters to everybody's needs equally up to infinity,
All his endeavors are for liberating us defines his
serenity;
By carving our lives he designs our destiny,
As infinity minus infinity is always equal to infinity.

God protects everyone of us from dangers equally up to
infinity,

Adversities he bestows on anyone are the part of his mercy;
He minimizes our mountain of sins to a small speck magically,
As infinity minus infinity is always equal to infinity.

He considers everybody's small piece of love equally as infinity,
Whether we offer leaf, flower or fruit he accepts each one whole heartedly;
He just wants our pure intentions to make us a part of his family,
As infinity minus infinity is always equal to infinity.

He accepts anybody's hatred also as love equally up to infinity,
Nothing can match the level of his divine tranquility;
Even the demons were delivered to his abode who criticized him openly,
As infinity minus infinity is always equal to infinity.

So what are we waiting to share this love equally with everyone up to infinity,
Even little efforts made on this path will count magnanimously;
And soon this will multiply with interest in the bank of

generosity,
As infinity minus infinity is always equals to infinity.
46

Dedication

Our mentors are like a compass who guide us at every step in life. They are an inspiration to reach great heights and our comfort when we get misdirected or feel dejected in life. So this book entitled "Spiritual Sails- A Souvenir for Life" is dedicated to my spiritual mentors who have motivated and guided me at each and every step holding hands due to which I am blessed today to share a collection of my poems with everyone who is reading this book in the entire globe.

Preface

Spirituality, an age old acquaintance of Indian culture, is a Vedic experiential science. With passage of time this concept has faded down the lane, but now-a-days this is re-emerging and is slowly creating a huge impact in lives of people. Spirituality is adding value in every perspective of life may it be mental, physical, family of financial and most important thing is that, it is preparing us for the unescapable truth of life i.e. Death. This has become a very powerful source of self improvement and is not only inculcating lost values in the growing civilization but is also helping to build a strong foundation for upcoming future generations to create a harmonious environment on this earth. In this book "Spiritual Sails- A Souvenir for Life", with blessings of Krishna and my mentors, I have tried to amalgamate the Vedic concepts, especially from Shrimad Bhagwad Geeta with topics of self improvement we commonly come across like mind management, anger management, self transformation, building harmonious relationships, tackling failures etc. and how to implement these concepts in practical life in an easy way. I have also tried to break some common myths that prevent us in taking up spirituality as a part of life, like devotion is for old age, it has nothing to do so with practical life and walking this path needs perfection in advance etc. Thus, for all those who are somewhere stuck in their lives, are stressed or want to make a comeback after a heart throbbing set back, this book can help them to overcome their situation and if this book will change any one person's life, I would be highly grateful to Lord Krishna for making me an instrument to spark the radiance of spirituality in his/her life.

So, without any further delay let's step on to a fresh journey of self improvement but this time with a beautiful tool of spirituality to make the process easy and materialized.

Acknowledgements

First and foremost, I would like to express my deepest gratitude to my best friend and my first spiritual mentor Dr. Shagun Mahajan for her invaluable motivation, support and constant encouragement throughout the duration of writing this book. I am highly obliged and indebted to my Spiritual Guru Dr. Nikhil Gupta Ji whose valuable teachings have guided me at every step during compilation of this book and it is only his inspiration and blessings that God made me capable to share his teachings with all those reading this book. I am extremely thankful to all my spiritual mentors Adv. Nitin Gupta ji, Smt. Preeti Gupta ji, Smt. Rupali Gupta ji, Sh. Nimish Gupta ji and the entire devotee association of my spiritual organization who have always been a source of positivity and strong motivation for me.

I would like to acknowledge my sister for her constant motivation and boosting spirit for completion of this book.

I would like to thank my Elementary School Mentors for building my strong base in language and inculcating in me writing as my hobby. Also, I would like to thank my parents and my brother who have been a constant support throughout the process.

Lastly, I am highly obliged to Book leaf Publications for providing a platform for a budding author like me to help me with getting my work published and giving the opportunity to everyone who want to progress further in this field.

Only to realize after, your pants
were reversed on your ass.
Or the time you made that stupid
comment,
I wish I knew the phrase and the
content.
Humiliating at that life stage,
Now, kind of a funny memory, I
gauge.

15. New Year's EVE Party 2025

OUTGOING opened the door to
the party,
and in walked FEAR, just a little
tardy.
They sat down by SHY, who
covered their face with a hat.
COURAGE noticed this and
walked over to chat.
FEAR was intimidated at first
glance.
But PATIENCE arrived, just by

chance.

FEAR nervously looked down at
the floor.

So, COURAGE took FEAR's hand,
saying no more.

Now FEAR, COURAGE, and
PATIENCE were hitting it off,

When along came
CONTRADICTION who rolled
their eyes with scoff.

WISDOM chimed in, "I love the
diversity."

Out of nowhere came PARADOX
showing acerbity.

CONTRADICTION knew
PARADOX so they ran to greet,

Everyone noticed......adorning
them.....AWE SWEEEEET!
SECRET was standing by the
punch bowl with MYSTERY; with
intense discretion.
When INTERRUPTION fell
through the ceiling, making quite
an impression!
LESS was a little rushed and
forgot to bring a dish to pass.
So, MORE was happy to share,
with all their character and class!
SHY gradually came out to
mingle,
Then LONELY accidentally
bumped COMPANION,

Who...... stated by, OBVIOUS, "Is
no longer single."

16. Letter to Future Me

I am writing a letter to future me.
Feels pretty weird to do
something so free.
I used to feel trapped, chains on
my wrists.
Feeling helpless and hopeless,
but here come some twists.
While now helpful and hopeful, I
am still grieving the living.
But now, with intention and
purpose, I DECIDE to be
GIVING.

Why let torture and anguish turn
my heart to stone?
I have aspirations and goals, yet
to be grown.
Do I dare tell you the future I
envision?
While fate, destiny, or chance
hijack; collision.
Can I please tell you what I want
in conclusion?
When, from the past, I know, it's
all an illusion.
Please hear me out, as I make a
request.
I promise to grow into myself,
with only me to impress.

As I do this with genuine amour,
and intention.
I ask that you guide me with
love, in my reflection.

17. EXPOSED

Exposed, one word, with so
many interpretations.
One showing openness, visibility,
and illumination.
Creating lovers, more intimate,
moreso flawless.
For them, it's the beauty of this
rawness.
Another meaning, the need for
protection from the elements.
Maybe from the brash snap of
winter, like the skin upon

elephants.

Maybe it's that flash of light

that's ruined a precious

photograph from years past.

While another, uses a photo as

blackmail, framed as something it

isn't...pureness to blast.

It's also vulnerability and

strength revealed.

However, when used against

someone, prompts a feeling to be

concealed.

Unmasked and unveiled, such a

wonderous thing.

Yet, unshielded and naked, create

feelings of shame that cling.

Out in the open, bare, or
unprotected.
With or without shelter,
undefended.
An unbelievable word, with so
much to explore.
EXPOSED you are, to richness of
words, more than before.

18. The Plane

You didn't know it, but that was
the exact moment I needed you.
Well, maybe not *YOU*, but you
were someone I already knew!
It was at that time I had lost
much of my hope.
Talking to you that night made it
easier for me to cope.

You see, it wasn't that I wasn't in
a good place.

But more that I was in a little

heartbroken space.

And through conversation, I

found that you were too.

Was fate pushing us together,

was this our cue?

You shared a little of your life

with me, maybe just a glimpse.

While I too, offered a piece of my

past, though I'm more of a wimp.

We continued to share stories,

feelings, times of hope and of

pain.

Our friendship, it started, I guess,

that night, on that plane.

Or...maybe before, when we

worked together.

That was a shitshow some days,
quite an adventure.

With few interactions, I still saw
who you were.

Kind and intelligent, though you
remembered it blurred.

Then I asked you to accompany
me to a show.

I had a great time, hilariously
awkward though.

We bonded over days at the gym,
building our muscles.

You, training for weightlifting,
me overcoming my mental
puzzles.

Who knows why our paths cross,
but I could guess that it's for life
to take a necessary pause, or
maybe even to share the pain of
loss.
But when we come together in
life as a friend, we tend to blend
our lives, which I highly
recommend!
Ok, logging off as this plane is
about to descend.

19. UNBROKEN

So, I've experienced my fair share
of trials and tribulations.
While getting to this point in my
life, at forty-five, I shudder with
lamentation.
For many things, I'm thankful
for, such as a safe, and loving
youth.
But as time lapsed into
adulthood, I noticed my decisions
which lacked couth.
Palpably, I started to see the

cracks in my decisions.
The life I created, walls closing
in, more and more restrictions.
Until I could no longer stand or
remember who I was.
My identity was shattered, from
gaslighting, a type of toxic scuzz.
A battle waged within; pressure
creating more creases.
Until I hit my breaking point,
fragments exploded into pieces.
But as I realize now, maybe that
was the way to become whole.
Maybe the only way to find
yourself again is to rediscover
your soul.

Maybe every choice we make is actually the path leading home. Turbulent, winding, and twisted, leading ultimately to *Shalom*. There were many points on this journey where I felt weak, words unspoken.

But I am stronger now, undeniably, forever and ever, UNBROKEN.

20. Racoon

It was the beginning of Mercury
Retrograde.

Let me paint the scene, get ready
for an escapade.

My friend, she works a job at a
yard, well underpaid.

When, one morning, arriving at
work, suddenly attacked, and
afraid.

She had reached down, to coil up
a hose, likely decayed.

And out of nowhere sprang a

racoon, like an unclipped
grenade.
Yelling for help, calling her
family, everyone was dismayed.
Now, off to the hospital, she must
masquerade.
Now getting a series of rabies
shots, so germs don't invade.
Her phone rings, her boss
demands a drug test, she is
shocked and feeling betrayed.
"Do drugs make racoons attack?"
Her boss remains un-swayed.
Anger and resentment bubble up
now, after working there over a
decade.

"I got the rabies shots and the
drug test," the message relayed.
She's wishing she could fry that
racoon, or maybe her boss,
sauteed.
Or maybe even get revenge,
(going too far...) or...strangulate.
Luckily, she is ultimately ok,
Stephanie...one to commemorate.

21. The Poetry Contest

Writing poems can be
exceptionally grand.
Unless you procrastinate, like me,
ideas unplanned.
I took the first step and entered
the contest festivity.
My creativity poured out, with
genuine authenticity.
With 21 poems to write in 21
days,
You know I waited until five days
left, my mind in a haze.

So, there I just started, putting
pen to the paper.
When I told my friends, I'm
guessing they wagered.
On if all of the poems I would
actually finish by deadline.
Or if I'd be calling and crying to
them on their friend hotline.
I thank my friends for the
inspiration to do this, I am
grateful.
I hope you all like some of my
poetry and find that it's tasteful!
Well, here it is, this is it, the
finish line.

Happy New Year's Eve, let's go have a glass of red wine!